DRAFTING YOUR
FINANCIAL
QUARTERBACK

DRAFTING YOUR FINANCIAL QUARTERBACK

What You Need to Know When Hiring a Financial Planner

Ryan Williamson, AIF®, CFP®

DRAFTING YOUR FINANCIAL QUARTERBACK

What You Need to Know When Hiring a Financial Planner

Full Disclosure:

The opinions voiced in this material are for general information only and are not intended to provide specific advice or recommendations for any individual. All performance referenced is historical and is no guarantee of future results. All indices are unmanaged and may not be invested into directly. This information is not intended to be a substitute for specific individualized tax or legal advice. We suggest that you discuss your specific situation with a qualified tax or legal advisor. Investing in mutual funds involves risk, including possible loss of principal. All investing involves risk including loss of principal. No strategy assures success or protects against loss. Securities offered through LPL Financial, Member FINRA/SIPC. Investment advice offered through Horizon Wealth Management, a registered investment advisor and separate entity from LPL Financial.

In collaboration with Bounce Solutions Publishing

Printed in the United States of America
IBSN: 9781726825436

Dedication

To my wife, Jami. Whether it's evening appointments, volunteering on the weekends, traveling to due diligence meetings or just working at home until 10pm, you have supported me throughout my entire career. Not only that, but you have built and created an amazing career of your own! I'm so proud of you. I love you Jami!

About the Author

Ryan Williamson is one of three founding partners of LaGrange, Illinois based investment firm Horizon Wealth Management. HWM was created to address the total financial picture of affluent individuals and their families. To do so effectively, HWM collaborates with a local network of tax, legal and estate planning experts for a full-service, integrated advisory practice.

Since 2000, Ryan has guided clients through multiple market cycles and major life events. His core competency is in the investment research used to develop asset management strategies employed at HWM. Ryan is also a CERTIFIED FINANCIAL PLANNER™ professional and an Accredited Investment Fiduciary (AIF®). He is the Compliance Officer of the firm ensuring all aspects of the practice are in accordance with the regulations of the Securities and Exchange Commission (SEC).

Ryan currently serves on the Boards of the LaGrange Business Association (Past President), the Legacy Guild (Executive Board) and the Chicago Zoological Society (Brookfield Zoo). He has been recognized for his excellence in the financial industry as a Five Star Wealth Manager* by Chicago Magazine for four years. He has also been a teacher through Lyons Township High School's Adult Education program for the past seven years.

Ryan lives in LaGrange, Illinois with his wife Jami and their two children Aidan and Alayna. In his (limited) free time, he enjoys exercising and playing guitar…having played in local cover bands for the past 6 years.

Table of Contents

Introduction

I wrote this to serve as a sound roadmap for those who have not worked with a Financial Advisor. For those who have, I want this to help validate the choice you've made or to expand your line of questioning when assessing your existing relationship.

Over the years, I am frequently asked about my motivation to do what I do. What is my "why" when it comes to providing financial advice? While I wish there was a drama laced, teary eyed tale to attribute it to, it candidly comes down to my own stubbornness and drive to succeed.

When I was in college a broker/dealer that I had been exposed to as a summer intern came on campus to interview seniors as they were hiring across the country. "Perfect!" I thought. So I jumped onto the computer's system to sign up for an open interview slot and received a message stating "you are not eligible to interview with this company." The actual message may have read differently, but you understand the point.

It turns out that since I was a Psychology major and NOT a Business major, I wasn't allowed to interview with the company. (Having been in the business for a long time now I can attest to the fact that I use my Psychology degree when helping clients manage their money/emotions much more than I would have used a Business degree).

I don't like the word "no." I decided at that point to go directly on the broker/dealer's website and apply on my own. A few interviews and 17 years later, here I am.

Over those years I've gained tremendous experience in the business. I've had some outstanding mentors that have helped educate me on intricate investments and planning strategies. I've had others help me take those strategies and present them to clients in a manner they understand.

I pride myself on being an advisor that doesn't use "broker language" when helping folks plan for what is most important to them. I look to write this book in a similar manner.

I also hope this is a due diligence piece for those who are and have worked with an Advisor before. You don't always know what you're not getting until someone hints that you might not be getting it. Since my career is built around asking and answering questions I figured that would be the most effective format for this book as well. And without further ado, let's get started.

Someone's sitting in the shade today because someone planted a tree a long time ago.
— Warren Buffet

Chapter 1

A Quarterback?

My favorite sport is football. Has been since I was a little kid. Growing up in Pittsburgh, football was in the DNA. It's an accessible city. I had Steelers' player's kids in my junior high classes.

I ran on the field of Three Rivers Stadium with my closest friends and still have an autographed football of some of the players during that time. One of the signatures is Louis Lipps, my favorite player of all time. He was a wide receiver, number 83. His claim to fame (at least for me) was when he caught a football…with his facemask!…and still scored a touchdown. It was unbelievable!

They now call it the Steel City Wonder. I never wanted to play wide receiver and never did, but he has always been my favorite player.

What did Louis Lipps need in order to be a successful receiver? Big hands and speed? Yes, good answer. Very true but not what I was thinking. He needed a quarterback to throw him the ball. Without the quarterback, there is no receiver!

Unfortunately for Louis Lipps, he played after Terry Bradshaw and before Ben Roethlisberger…the two greatest Steelers quarterbacks of all time and quite frankly, two of the best who have ever played the game.

So, who was his quarterback? During the time I lived in Pittsburgh he had two: Mark Malone and Bubby Brister. And other than Mark Malone looking like Tom Selleck, these are two names that most people outside of Steeler Nation have rarely heard.

Throughout history, it can be demonstrated that the quarterback position is one of, if not the, most important position on the football field. They are charged with scanning the defense to look for potential risks of the called play. If they see something they don't like, they audible the play…hopefully with a positive result.

The QB leads the other skilled players; telling them where to run their routes, which defender to block, and how best to march the ball down the field to put points on the board. The QB often gains the glory when they win but more dramatically are viewed as responsible when they lose.

No matter the outcome of the game and the corresponding public response, the QB must stay focused on what he's doing, how he's leading the team and go out and do it again the following week. In my opinion, it is one of the most difficult positions in all of sports.

A quarterback takes considerable physical punishment while keeping their mental focus crystal clear. They must study every aspect of the game, learn how to pick up queues in the middle of a game and make fast, on the spot adjustments accordingly. They enter each contest with a game plan yet by halftime, the plan evolves based on the real life situation.

You should view your Financial Advisor as a Financial Quarterback. Your QB is tasked with working through the game plan that gives you the greatest chance of success. In every situation, your game plan will require audibles as time goes on. The markets may become volatile when not expected. Tax law changes may impact how efficient your investments become. International relationships may weaken and challenge the very fabric of our global economy. These are all factors that cannot be built into an initial financial plan.

However, the right Financial Quarterback will help in changing the script so that these unexpected circumstances don't become catastrophic to your long-term strategy.

Your Financial QB can also help your other position players (accountant, estate planning attorney, insurance agent) by working with them on how best to game plan collectively on your behalf.

And just like the Pittsburgh Steelers (or your favorite NFL team), you have the opportunity to "draft" the right Financial Quarterback for your situation and personality. You don't have to settle on one that isn't the best leader for your financial needs.

The goal of this book is to give you pre-draft information that will help clarify what to look for when interviewing financial advisors. I will stress that interviewing a few professionals is the best way to find the right one for you.

Think of buying your next car. Most of us won't do so before test driving a few to experience the differences firsthand…sometimes more than once. I would absolutely hope you approach the hiring of your Financial Quarterback with the same tenacity and patience! You want this to be a long-term relationship where you are provided guidance through the evolution of your financial life. Take the process seriously.

Money is only a tool. It will take you wherever you wish,
but it will not replace you as the driver.
– Ayn Rand

Chapter 2

What makes you, the reader, a good client?

You may be thinking that of all the possible topics I could have started the meat of this book with, choosing this one is a bit odd. It might be…but it isn't.

Throughout, this book I'll help you prepare for an interview with a potential advisor or analyze your current advisor situation to make sure it's the right fit. I will primarily focus on what you could and should expect from the right professional partner.

However, just because the advisor might check all the boxes I will walk through in this book, doesn't mean you are also an appropriate fit for them. I mean no disrespect by this statement. I'm actually trying to help you avoid spending time on something that may not make sense for *you*. The last thing I want is for you to read this book, sit back and say, "you know, I don't think this book even applied to me."

Just because there are pool mechanics out there, doesn't mean you need a pool…or a mechanic for that pool…even though you might like to swim on hot days. Maybe you like to watch instructional videos and try to fix your pool yourself.

Similarly, there are many groups that provide financial services…banks, insurance agents, financial advisors, accountants, etc. But just because they exist doesn't mean you need them. However, if you were someone who truly needs a financial advisor (like most of us), let me tell you what will (or does) make you a good client.

Wait, I'm calling an audible. I think it's actually more entertaining if I tell you what DOESN'T make you a good client.

First, my disclaimer. Over the past 17+ years I've worked with hundreds and hundreds of clients. I appreciate them all and thank them for their confidence in me. One of the best parts of my job is that each client is unique. Not all meetings or phone calls are alike. My clients are great people and great clients.

The types of clients I reference as "not great" are only not great because they get in their own way of financial success. They either don't listen to guidance and advice or don't fully trust the process.

When you watch money shows on TV, the hosts do not know your situation and are not making recommendations that suit YOUR needs. They give general ideas; not ones that should be followed blindly.

Take their advice in context. The ideas advisors suggest for their clients are based on personal circumstances and all the information gathered over hours of consultation.

The people who look to mass media for investment advice aren't great clients. Though I do love engaging clients on ideas or thoughts they've heard from other sources…like the media. But if in the end they make a decision based more on what they've heard than the personal work we've done together, they are getting in their own way.

Similarly, getting financial advice from a friend, neighbor, relative or co-worker who believes they've cracked the code on successful investing may not be the best investment strategy. I'm sure there are plenty of times throughout history where a very good investment suggestion was passed at a neighborhood block party, but I assume that many of these shared ideas were grabbed from the media (my first point).

Let me explain a bit by telling a real-world story from my career.

We've all heard the term "buy high and sell low." For investors, it's the number one rule NOT to follow! There is absolutely a psychology to this phenomenon. It's real and it's ugly. I liken it to the "fair weather fan" syndrome. When a team is hot, we all become fans. We want to see their games live, buy their bumper sticker, tattoo their captain's name on our shoulder.

When are prices at their peak? When everyone else wants the same thing we do! When do people sell their investments? When everyone else is! And when is that? Usually when the prices are low.

As humans we tend to follow the herd...psychologists Gabriel Tarde and Gustave Le Bon actually coined this thought in the 19th century.

I began my career in late 2000. While I remember the tail end of the tech bubble (investments I was suggesting to clients had 100+% return over the previous twelve months) I wasn't seasoned enough with my clients to have learned their tendencies. We all remember the tech bubble bursting and the pain felt in stock market investments.

The next bubble we saw after this was in real estate. Historically, real estate is an investment designed to grow a bit over time but primarily to keep you ahead of inflation. Oh, it's also supposed to be your home where you create memories, raise a family, etc. That all changed in the mid-2000s.

I work with clients of all ages but a good majority of my clients are retirees who are 60 and older. Traditionally, these clients are a bit more conservative with their investments. If they are on a fixed income, even more so. It was around 2006 (a year before the real estate catastrophe) and I received a call from one of my more conservative, retired clients. She was a sweet woman I'd been working with for close to 5 years at this point and my focus for her was income with moderate growth. That just means that her main need from her assets invested with me was income with a secondary goal of inflation protection through growth.

She was 75, a widow and had 2 kids with 6 grandkids. Her family dynamic isn't of consequence, but it helps paint the picture of who she was. That day she called and said she wanted to take a large sum of money out of her account with me. Large distributions were very unlike her.

At this point I typically prefer a meeting face to face in order to make sure I fully understand what she's looking to do and that she fully understands how her decisions may impact her long-term plan. When we met I uncovered the fact that she had heard from a friend about a real estate investment idea that, in my opinion, seemed too good to be true…at a time when everyone seemed to want it. This is the process I enjoy the most because we had an open and honest conversation about her priorities, her risk tolerance, and her short, intermediate and long-term goals. Through this conversation she decided that it was best for her to hold off on chasing her friend's investment idea. She did not get in her own way but did take an idea and talked through it with her professional advisor. She avoided becoming a 'not great client.'

She was a great client for another 10 years before she passed away. She believed in my process…our process…and that my primary role was to guide her financially.

From a greater perspective, how can an advisor help clients from getting in their own way when it comes to investment decisions? To explain, I'll start with an analogy. My biggest control issue is in driving the car. I don't ride. I won't ride. I need to be the driver. I've driven so many types of cars because no matter who I'm with, I drive the car. One day, my partner came into the office with a moving violation ticket from a crime he didn't remember committing. It had a picture of his license plate…so it was definitely his car.

After 15 minutes, we put together that I was actually the one driving *his* car from a meeting we were at when I "rolled" a stop light. I paid him for it, but it was a funny reminder of my insistence of driving. Why must I drive? The control, yes. But it's because as the driver, you know what's coming ahead of you. You know why the car might be bumping around a bit. You know whether the drive is going to call for slamming on the brakes. As a passenger, you aren't privy to this info. You just believe and have faith that the driver will get you where you want to go safely.

In my opinion, even worse than being a car passenger is being an airplane passenger. You can't see in front of you and have no idea what's ahead.

For me, being a market investor is like being an airplane passenger. When the flight gets bumpy and volatile, I can't get off the plane fast enough. When the markets go through bumpy volatility, some investors can't get out fast enough. They don't know what's ahead and uncertainty is scary.

Often it's harder to keep people from selling in tough times than it is to keep them from buying in times of euphoria. Fear is a stronger emotion than greed. My best clients use these opportunities to vent, express their concerns, remind me how much they rely on that money, inform me what they'll do to me if it's all lost, **but what they do not do is sell**. "Not so great clients" let their emotions blur the long term while focusing on the right now!

I've used some observations from my experience to demonstrate how clients can and have gotten in their own way. Sometimes they rely upon sources like the media or their friends because they've not yet found a person they trust with those decisions. Other times they respond like the herd during different market cycles.

In the end, though, they see the forest through the trees and believe in the bigger picture.

If you are one of these people, I really encourage you to continue the search for your Financial QB!

Financial peace isn't the acquisition of stuff. It's learning to live on less than you make, so you can give money back and have money to invest. You can't win until you do this.
— Dave Ramsey

Chapter 3

Designation Nation

When I say, "Physical Therapist," what do you think of? For me, I think of many things. I think of people seeking one in hopes of relief from an injury. I see exercise equipment, massage tables, and stretching techniques. I hear another professional telling someone "you need to see a physical therapist if you want full range of motion in your shoulder again." There is crystal clear clarity in what this profession is, what people go to them for, and what the desired results look like. I believe it would be very difficult for me to see a physical therapist and walk out thinking "boy, that person doesn't do anything I thought they would."

Now, what do you think of when I say "Investment Consultant?" Or how about "Financial Planner?" Or how about "Investment Advisor Representative?" "Wealth Manager?" "Financial Consultant?" "Registered Representative?" As a bonus, what if I started throwing acronyms after the name? AAMS. AWMA. ChFC. CFP®. AIF®. MPAS. CIPM. CIMA.

When you have a minute, go to FINRA.org (FINRA stands for Financial Industry Regulatory Authority). On that website, you'll find 183 different acronyms...1 for each designation that a Financial Advisor can obtain and put after their name on their business cards.

So I'll ask you the question. If you saw two names; 1) John Doe, CFA, CMFC/Investment Broker and 2) Jim Doe, CFP®, CFDP/Registered Representative, what would you expect by walking into each office? Would you have the same experience? Would John and Jim provide the same services using a similar philosophy?

One thing about my industry is that it's very easy for us to use names and designations to impress the public and potential clients.

Over my 18-year career I've earned 4 designations myself, so I am certainly not immune. However, the point of this chapter is to help you understand the differences so that when you see the array of titles and designations, you have a better understanding of what to expect from the professionals that have them.

Will I go through all the titles AND every one of the 183 designations? No I won't. Many of them you may never come across. I'm about efficiency and effectiveness and will only cover the most common.

TITLES

As I mentioned above, there are quite a few ways that financial professionals can describe themselves. If I'm a Physical Therapist…I'm a Physical Therapist. If I'm a financial advisor, I can select one of many names. Let's talk through some of the main ones:

1) **Financial Advisor**: this is one of the most common and broad stroke titles there is. By definition, a

financial advisor is a professional who suggests and renders financial services to clients based on their financial situation.

I feel that if you look up "vague" in the dictionary, the picture of a financial advisor should help illustrate it. According to FINRA (one of the main regulatory bodies in our industry), the following professional groups may use the term financial advisor: brokers, investment advisers, accountants, lawyers, insurance agents and financial planners. Clear as mud?

2) **Wealth Manager**: by name, this is one of the clearest titles and easiest to understand. I would assume that when I walk into a Wealth Manager's office, they will help me manage my wealth. Simple.
Actually, this is a complex position. Wealth managers incorporate financial planning, investment management, retail banking, estate planning, tax planning, and other areas into their client relationships.

They focus primarily on High Net Worth Individuals and business owners. Wealth Managers are not a group that's right for everyone as they typically handle complex planning and management for families with significant wealth.

3) **Investment Advisor Representative**: these professionals are registered with the Securities and Exchange Commission (SEC) or a state's securities

agency. The SEC is the other main regulatory body along with FINRA.

IARs are defined as an individual or a firm that is in the business of giving advice about securities and managing client accounts more. The IAR's work with or for a Registered Investment Advisor (RIA). An RIA is a firm engaged in the activities detailed above. RIAs, though, have a fiduciary duty to their clients. That means they have the obligation to provide suitable investment advice and always act in the best interests of their clients.

4) **Stockbroker**: this is an older term that isn't nearly as common as it was a few decades ago. However, I wanted to point this name out because it can be buried under the "Financial Advisor" title.
It's not quite as difficult to find one of these as it is to find Bigfoot, but it's not far off. The general definition of a Stockbroker is a broker who buys and sells securities on a stock exchange on behalf of clients.

DESIGNATIONS

All of the above titles require appropriate licensing to operate their business. No matter what type of financial professional you work with, they have passed licensing tests in order to conduct business.

I give credit to any advisor who believes in their business and values education enough to spend the time and money necessary to obtain non-essential designations. I won't discount or discredit any of them.

Personally, however, I believe a handful demonstrate credentials that should make clients feel more comfortable with that professional.

In full disclosure, I have two of the three designations I detail below. I decided to earn them because of the experience I've gained over my career and what I've found to be most important to potential and existing clients.

I compare advisors with designations to Peyton Manning. While I'm not a big fan of his (though I think he's quite entertaining in the Nationwide commercials), I respect him. Yes he was a football player. But he was special because he was always learning. He never felt that he knew it all.

Advisors with designations continue to learn. They are required to put hours in each year to maintain the designations. They are the Peyton Manning's of the investment industry!

DESIGNATIONS

1. **AIF® – *Accredited Investment Fiduciary*.** A fiduciary by definition is a person who holds a legal or ethical relationship of trust with one or more other parties.

   It also means that the advisor must do his or her best to make sure investment advice is made using accurate and complete information, or simply, that the analysis is as thorough and accurate as possible.

   Avoiding conflicts of interest is important when acting as a fiduciary, and it means that an advisor must disclose any potential conflicts to placing the client's interests ahead of the advisors.

This designation allows me (and other advisors who've obtained it) to attest that I believe in being a fiduciary for my clients.

2. **CFA** – *Chartered Financial Analyst*. I have a tremendous amount of respect for those who've obtained this one because it seems like an absolutely grueling process! It reminds me of two-a-day football practices…but this has *three* parts! The three levels of exams cover areas such as accounting, economics, ethics, money management and security analysis.

The exams are offered only twice per year. If you don't pass the first time, you wait at least six months for a second chance. According to the CFA Institute, the most recent (June, 2017) pass rates for the three exams are: Level 1: 43%, Level 2: 47% and Level 3: 54%.

This is not a designation you decide you want to obtain on Monday and earn it heading into the weekend. There is a tremendous amount of commitment and time to earn and maintain this designation. Talk about brutal…hats off to you CFAs!

3. **CFP® – *CERTIFIED FINANCIAL PLANNER*™.** With as much respect as I have for the designation previously mentioned (CFA), I feel

the CFP® is more relevant to personal financial planning.

The first step to CFP® certification is completing CFP® Board education requirements in the major personal financial planning areas, including:

a. Professional Conduct and Regulation
b. General Principles of Financial Planning
c. Education Planning
d. Risk Management and Insurance Planning
e. Investment Planning
f. Tax Planning
g. Retirement Savings and Income Planning
h. Estate Planning
i. Financial Plan Development

After completing the necessary coursework, it's time for the exam. The exam consists of two 3-hour sessions separated by a scheduled 40-minute halftime.

FINAL POINT

With the number of people holding themselves out as financial advisors, it behooves you to understand some of the basic differences right out of the gates.

The most important characteristics of your advisor are; experience, trust, integrity, knowledge, and honesty. Unfortunately, none of the above designations can absolutely guarantee that a professional will possess these characteristics. However, when speaking with an advisor you now know what to ask about their credentials and those answers will help in building your comfort level.

I made my money the old fashioned way. I was very nice to a wealthy relative right before he died.
- Malcolm Forbes

Chapter 4

How is your Financial QB paid?

To this point, you've ensured that you are a good client who is seeking professional guidance for the right reasons.

You also have much more clarity about how to differentiate between the many professionals competing for your business. You've narrowed the list to your top three candidates and set up appointments to meet with them individually. Now what?

While this chapter is about advisor compensation and how we're paid, I want to digress a bit. Yes, you want to work with an advisor who has all the credentials and experience that is important to you.

You want to believe that they are working for you and your best interests. You also hope they believe enough in their practice to continue their education and to stay current on industry changes that will impact you and your financial situation.

Once you find the ideal advisor who checks all those boxes, you will have a great advisor on your team. But are these the most important details?

My clients know I demonstrate all of the above characteristics. I've been in business since 2000, I have credentials, I'm a fiduciary, I attend industry workshops, and I complete my continuing education each year.

Now, let me tell you why I don't work with every person I've met.

I had a Stonehenge Bulldog that we unfortunately had to put down at the ripe old age of 13. Stonehenge Bulldog are ½ English Bulldog and ½ American Bulldog. I loved that dog. That dog hated other dogs. We took her to training, had specialists in our home and did hours of research. Nothing worked, she still hated other dogs.

Throughout her life we crossed the street if another dog was walking in our direction. We never visited dog parks. We could never bring her to family or friend's homes who also had dogs. It was sad.

I'll never forget what the last specialist we worked with told me. She said "dogs are like people. They don't have to like everybody."

Dogs are like people, they don't have to like everybody. You are a client and you don't have to like every financial advisor. **Do not** ignore your gut feeling to the professional with whom you meet.

They may have all the credentials in the world but if they come across in a way that doesn't sit right with you personally, they are not the right fit for you. I love telling people how my client meetings look. If they last an hour, we talk for 20 minutes about their planning and investments and 40 minutes about our families, current events, etc.

It's a bond and a kinship that goes far deeper than how well their accounts are performing. When you see your advisors name and number appear on your caller ID, you want to have an immediate, positive response. Long story short, you want to like your advisor, personally. There are too many of us out there to work with someone where there's not a personal connection.

So now back to the point of this chapter and how you might pay your Financial QB.

One of the first questions any prospective client asks me is about my compensation. I am transparent about my fees because I don't want them to be a roadblock that gets in the way of their financial success. If you don't get a straight answer to this question when asking it, warning flags should be raised.

Your financial quarterback will never forget the golden rule; we are working with YOUR money on YOUR behalf. That means YOU can take it wherever you want it to be managed by whomever you want. There are no commitments or contracts with advisors.

There are three main ways that financial advisors are compensated for their services and sometimes it can be a combination of a couple of them.

1. Commissions
2. Advisory fee
3. Flat/Planning fee

Or, again, a combination of a couple of them.

The first possible form of compensation is through commissions. This is the oldest form of compensation and for many, many years was the only option available.

How it works is like this: if there's a transaction made in your account, there is a commission paid to the advisor. Simple as that. If you wanted to buy 100 shares of your favorite stock, the advisor is happy to oblige…with a commission added to the transaction.

Typically, the commission on a stock trade is based on a couple things: how many shares you are buying or selling and the price per share of the stock.

I would tell clients that the commission on a stock trade is between 1 and 1.5% of the overall total. So if you were buying $500,000 of a stock, the commission would (most likely) be $5,000-$7,000.

What about mutual funds? According to Statista.com, as of the end of 2016 there were over $16 trillion in mutual fund assets.

It's worth knowing how commissions work with mutual funds because of their prominence in the industry. There are two ways to invest in mutual funds. Right now I'm focusing on how it works when commissions are involved in the transaction.

In order to do that simply I will refer to this as the alphabet soup of mutual funds. There are different ways to buy into them and so there are differences in the fee structures.

Mutual funds have different share classes. No matter which share class you invest in, you're investing in the same stocks, bonds or combination of both as you would in the other share classes. The main difference is the fee structure.

A Shares. These are mutual funds that have an up-front sales charge. Think of it as a signing bonus for the advisor.

Many fund companies have up-front sales charges as high as 5.75%. Easy math: for every $100,000 you invest, $5,750 is immediately taken as a fee so you are actually investing only $94,250 into the fund. 5% of this will go to the advisor and 0.75% will go to the fund company.

Funds DO have quantity discounts so depending on how much you're investing in the same mutual fund company, the 5.75% can be reduced to 4%, 3%, 2% or even 0%. Since you paid the fee up front, the money is liquid to you the very next day. If you wanted to sell the fund a month from when you bought it, you can do so with no penalty. The money is yours!

B Shares. These are mutual funds that do NOT have an up-front sales charge. However, they have what are called back-end charges. Using the example above, if you wanted to sell this fund a month after you bought it, there would be a penalty to do so. Sometimes a significant penalty (7% or more). That "penalty" charge is lowered each year until eventually going to 0%, but it could take 7 years before you can get 100% of your money back.

Now, how is the advisor paid if there's no up-front sales charge? Great question! They are paid 4% right way...but it isn't taken out of the proceeds.

If you invest $100,000 into a mutual fund B share, $100,000 is invested and goes to work for you right away. And $4,000 goes to the advisor on day 1. One of the main reasons that there is a back-end charge on these funds is so the fund company can recoup the commissions paid to the advisor up front.

C Shares. These have no up-front sales charges. They do, however, have a 12 month back-end charge of 1%. In month 13, the money is all yours. The advisor is paid 1% at the time of transaction (hence the 1% back end charge).

So, if you invest $100,000, the full $100,000 is invested, the advisor earns $1,000, and the money should stay in the fund for 12 months in order to avoid a 1% penalty.

12b-1. What the heck is this? I can easily argue that there's a small b in it so it still fits in my alphabet analogy. These are ongoing fees paid to the advisor. Unlike up-front and back-end charges, they are built into the internal expenses of ALL mutual fund share classes mentioned above. You don't see them. Consider these to be the "salary" of the advisor.

NFL quarterbacks are sometimes paid a signing bonus (up-front sales charge). Sometimes they forego some of their compensation due to injury or trade (back-end charges). They are always paid an annual salary (12b-1 fees).

Obviously with the A shares the advisor gets the biggest signing bonus because they receive the largest check up front. However, they have the lowest annual salary going forward. The 12b-1 of an A share is typically 0.25%. The signing bonus for an advisor using C shares is the lowest at 1%. However, the salary (12b-1) is 1% a year.

Now you have a basic understanding of how commissions work.

By law, advisors who work on commissions are operating in a sales capacity. Their main guiding principal is KYC...Know Your Customer.

Their job is to know their client's situation and make investment recommendations that they believe to be appropriate. They are paid for the transactions made.

Let's move to the other side of the spectrum and look at the second potential compensation structure; paying an advisory fee or what's commonly referred to as a "wrap fee."

This compensation is not investment specific, its account specific. What I mean by that is that the wrap fee is assessed to the value of the account no matter what investments are held within it.

The wrap fee charged by most advisors will range from 0.5% to 1.5% of the total account value. If we assume a 1% wrap fee and an account of $250,000, the advisor would be paid $2500 a year.

There are significant differences between this compensation structure and the commission based one I discussed first. The main one is that there are NO sales charges with the mutual funds. There are also NO 12b-1 fees.

There actually are completely different share classes of funds for this structure to reflect the lack of these fees. Typically, you'll see them as "I shares" or "F shares."

There are also NO commissions when buying or selling a stock. If you bought $500,000 of a stock, $500,000 is invested into that stock. Why is that? Because the advisor is being compensated an annual fee based on the value of your account.

This leads to the next difference. Since the advisors' compensation is a fee based on your account, their compensation is impacted by your account's performance. If your account goes up in value, their compensation goes up. However, if your account loses value, your advisors' paycheck also gets smaller. Wouldn't we like this in our NFL quarterback?

As I mentioned I'm from Pittsburgh but now live outside of Chicago. Jay Cutler is a quarterback of recent history for the Chicago Bears. Let's say Jay had one of his 0 touchdown and 4 interception football games.

Many fans would have loved to see him lose part of his salary! Now if he led the Bears to a 16-win season, they would have gladly watched his salary increase with each win! A fee-based advisors' compensation works the same way.

These fees are considered "advisory" fees because by law, you are paying the advisor for their advice, not the transactions. This requires them to work as a fiduciary. These fees are 100% transparent, meaning you'll always know what your advisor is paid. There is no head scratching or muddled responses when asked "well how much do you pay your advisor?"

Now let's say you're not interested in having an advisor manage your assets for you. Or let's say you want to see how they approach your financial big picture through planning before you decide whether or not you feel comfortable with them managing the assets.

If either of these are the case, you can also pay the planner to construct a financial roadmap for you. This is the third method of compensation referenced as a flat fee or planning fee.

Whether it's longer term retirement planning, clear and present college planning, or a combination of those and other topics, some advisors can create this reporting for a fee. Think of it like buying the game script but not the in-game coaching.

The advisor/planner will map where you are, what your goals are, the most effective strategies to getting there, and the potential risks that may keep you from success. *For more specifics of what the planner can do, please go back and reference the areas of focus under CFP® in the previous chapter.*

With this structure, you walk out of the office with a manual of how to coach the game. You will have probabilities of success, suggestions on how to increase those chances, and areas of weakness that should be addressed. However, you are the coach and are responsible for putting together the right lineup on the field, making the in-game adjustments, and updating the game plan as life dictates.

Some advisors bill hourly for this work. However, most that I've come across (including myself) will bill a flat fee.

No matter which way you choose to pay to work with an advisor, it's good to know you have options.

While there is rigidity in this business, there is flexibility with whom you work and how you pay them for that work. And after you decide which structure is right for you, you can change structures at any point as there are no contracts nor restrictions. My suggestion is to understand your needs, values and goals while choosing the right advisor that works within the appropriate compensation structure to help lead you towards your financial success.

I never attempt to make money on the stock market. I buy on the assumption that they could close the market the next day and not reopen it for ten years.
– Warren Buffet

Chapter 5

What investments might your Financial QB suggest for you?

One of the ways advisors are different from quarterbacks is in the number of tools they use when they're working. A quarterback has one…a football.

No matter what the weather is or how many points they're down or what offensive lineman got injured, they have one thing to use: the football.

Advisors have the benefit of being able to use many types of "footballs." Ones that will go long for the Hail Mary. Ones that will keep it short and safe. Ones that will protect against inclement environments.

Your trust is in the fact that your financial quarterback will use the right ball given your situation and the flow of the game.

This chapter in and of itself could be a book. However, I respect your time and will keep it concise.

Because of my respect of your time, there are many more investment vehicles than what I discuss. But why mention obscure options that might make sense for 0.3% of the investing population? Instead I'll cover the main investments advisors will use, a basic description of them, and some questions surrounding each that you should ask.

Stocks: the flagship and cornerstone of investments. Most people know what these are, have owned them in one form or another, and talk about them with their friends. Stocks are the easiest investment to grow a personal attachment to.

I have personal experience with a stock and how closely attached one can become with them. My grandfather retired from one of the major employers located in Detroit, Michigan. Over the years, this company provided so much for my family.

That company helped pay for my father and his sibling's college educations. It helped my grandparents support and raise 5 children. It was more than a company to my family, it was a financial giving tree that helped them in immeasurable ways.

At a challenging time in our nations' history, they filed bankruptcy and wiped out a pretty significant chunk of my grandma's pension. Even still, we have an attachment to that stock that is much deeper than what its price is any given day.

So what is a stock? It's an ownership share of a public company. If you own a share of a company, you are part owner OF that company.

Your stock in the company will go up or down based on how the company is doing. How many cars have they sold? Is it more or less than last year? Is management leading the company in the right direction? As a stock owner, you are part of this journey.

There are many different types of stocks that you can invest in. Some are in growth companies that look to create the next best technology. Some are stodgy, long tenured companies that are used more for dividends and provide us with our basic need products. Some are small companies in foreign countries that might benefit as the demand for the product increases along with wealth of the population.

For details and specifics of the different types of stocks and when best they should be used, I suggest consulting with your advisor. And when you do so, here are a few questions that may help you understand what you're investing in:

1. What type of company is this?
2. What industry are they in?
3. Why do you believe them to be better than their competition?
4. Is it smart to own only one company?
5. What if they file for bankruptcy?
6. Will I lose my money?
7. How far will it go down before you suggest that we sell out of it?
8. How high will it go before you suggest that we take our gains?
9. How often do you buy and sell stocks?
10. How does this stock fit into the rest of my portfolio?

Bonds: many investors view these as the opposite of stocks. They use bonds because they will historically go up when stocks go down. It's a way to diversify away from the risks of owning stocks. Much more difficult to become personally attached to.

Quite honestly, I don't have any stories that can paint bonds in the same light as stocks. Ok, I guess I have one.

For all the Chicago Bears fans out there, you may remember when they redid Soldier Field. They spent hundreds of millions of dollars renovating the stadium, adding new seats and making it a better experience for fans. Who paid for that? Partially, investors. How?

They invested in Soldier Field Bonds. Bonds were issued to help raise money for the project. So for some Bears fans, their money went towards helping their favorite team build a better, yet uglier, stadium. (Sorry, my personal opinion about how it looks…no offense meant).

So what is a bond? A bond is a debt instrument where you are loaning your money to a company, government, sports team, etc.

Unlike a stock where you are an owner of the company, with a bond you are a debtor of the company. When a company (or football team) needs to raise money, many times they will issue bonds in order to do so. When you invest in a bond, let's say $500,000, you are loaning them your money for a specified and fixed period of time…say 5 years. In return, you are expecting interest payments based on the bond's coupon, or fixed interest rate.

Bonds have different coupons based on the company and how strong they are financially.

For easy math let's say you invested in a 5% bond. You would invest $500,000 and would look to receive fixed payments of 5% each year while you own the bond. They can't change the interest rate so you are locked in at that 5%. Each bond also has a maturity…when the bond will end.

Let's say this bond matured in 10 years. For 10 years, your $500,000 bond would pay 5% interest each year. After 10 years, you expect to receive your $500,000 back.

Relatively easy concept. However, there are different risks with bonds than stocks: interest rate risk, default risk, credit risk, inflation risk and market risk.

Below are questions to ask your advisor about these investments:

1. How do the abovementioned risks impact this bond?
2. How long until this bond matures?
3. What is the credit rating of the issuer of this bond?
4. Is it a taxable or tax free bond?
5. What is the price of the bond?
6. Is it trading at a discount or a premium?
7. How frequently are the coupon payments paid? Monthly? Quarterly? Semi-annually?
8. Is the bond callable? (This means the company would have the ability to pay you back BEFORE the stated maturity).

Mutual Funds: now that we've covered the basics of stocks and bonds, we can migrate into mutual funds.

A mutual fund is an investment where a money manager selects stocks, bonds and other investments and wraps them into one packaged product.

The analogy I use with prospective clients involves a grocery cart. Let's say you're in a grocery store and you pick up a box of your favorite cereal for the kids. In the cart it goes.

You then pick up some shampoo because you believe in your personal hygiene, to the delight of your coworkers.

Walking through the store is making you hungry…so you grab a big bag of nacho cheese chips. And now you need to wash your orange stained hands so you find the best smelling bottle of hand soap!

You look down in your cart and you see four unrelated products produced by four different companies. This is a mutual fund! Instead of putting all your money into one company or brand, you gain exposure to many through diversification. The grocery cart is the mutual fund. The fund manager decides what companies they want in it and which ones they don't.

As I mentioned above, mutual funds can have a combination of many different types of investments; stocks, bonds, commodities (like oil or steel), currencies, real estate, etc.

When you know what you want your investment portfolio to look like, or better yet, when your financial quarterback helps you put together the appropriate investment strategy, you'll have a better understanding of which type(s) of mutual funds to use and why.

Through that process, the below questions will help you understand and select the appropriate solution:

1. How is the fund invested and what types of investments can the manager use?
2. How long has the manager been overseeing the fund? (Experience can be important).
3. How big or small is the mutual fund? Sometimes they can be too big and sometimes too small.
4. What are the fees associated with the fund?

5. What fees will I see and what fees will I not?
6. Is there a penalty to sell?
7. How has it performed in relation to its peers?
8. Do you (the advisor) receive special treatment or compensation by recommending a specific mutual fund company?
9. How often do you analyze the mutual fund to make sure it is still the appropriate one to own?

ETFs (Exchange Traded Funds): these have gained tremendous popularity over the past few years. I typically describe these as a combination of a stock and a mutual fund.

They trade like stocks…meaning you can buy and sell them at any point during the day when the markets are open (between 8:30am and 3pm CST). In comparison, mutual funds trade only once per day AFTER the market closes.

However, ETFs act like mutual funds because they are a basket of many investments in one holding.

The difference is that, there aren't managers actively managing the investments within the ETF like there are with mutual funds. The investments are typically selected and reviewed periodically…maybe quarterly, semiannually or annually…and adjusted at that point. Because of that, the expenses are typically lower because you're on the boat without paying for a full-time captain.

ETFs can have a very strong position in your portfolios and before implementing them, ask these questions:

1. Is this ETF based solely on an index (the health care index, for instance) or is it diversified amongst many areas?
2. What are the expenses? What does it cost for me to buy them?
3. How is it "managed" or adjusted?
4. Should I use ETFs for stock –type investments or bond-type investments? Or both?
5. Should ETFs be a core holding in my portfolio or may they be better served as a smaller, satellite holding?

Other Investments: There are many other types of investments that may be presented to you. Above, I covered the most commonly owned. Others that I didn't detail are:

1. Annuities (Fixed, Variable, Equity Index)
2. Non Traded REITs (Real Estate Investment Trusts)
3. Unit Investment Trusts (UITs)
4. Hedge Funds
5. Fund of Funds
6. Derivatives
7. Options
8. And many, many more!

There is no shortage of ways to invest your money, just like there are no shortages of plays that a football team can use.

The role of the quarterback is to read the defense and call the most appropriate play in any given situation.

Your financial quarterback will read your defense to make the recommendations. By "your defense" I mean your time horizon, risk tolerance, short-mid-long-term goals, tax situation, investment experience, etc.

Picking an investment is more than buying something you heard your friend talk about. It's looking at the entire game plan as well as the current situation to determine the best mix of the above options.

I love money. I love everything about it. I bought
some pretty good stuff. Got me a $300 pair of socks.
Got a fur sink. An electric dog polisher. A gasoline
powered turtleneck sweater. And, of course,
I bought some dumb stuff, too.
– Steve Martin

Chapter 6

Constructing your financial game plan

In my opinion, the most important role of your financial quarterback is putting together a plan that helps tie it all together. I talked a lot about the tools available to them in the form of investments. Quite frankly, they really won't know which tools to use unless they know what those tools are designed to build.

Any NFL quarterback conducts most of their work behind the scenes. We see them on Sunday (or Monday, or Thursday) when they're in "game mode."

What we don't see is the hundreds of hours they put in each week on the practice field, in the gym and in the film room. They also spend a lot of time focusing on their diets, their sleep habits, their mental health, etc.

A Financial Advisor does the same thing (without forced exercise, physical contact and ice baths). Most of the work they do is behind the scenes. After getting to know who you are, what your goals are, what your risk tolerance is, and other pertinent financial and personal information, they work for hours on creating an appropriate game plan for you.

This not only involves your specific case, but it involves a holistic knowledge of the industry, the laws that impact investments, taxes and estates, effective strategies for short, mid and long-term goal planning and anything else that has to do with money.

Below is information on how your financial quarterback will game plan for your most critical life events.

Retirement Planning:

The MVP of the planning world, retirement is the largest expense we will face as individuals. **The biggest fear amongst the pre-retirees and retirees I work with is outliving their money.**

I'm sure this concern isn't isolated to my practice as this theme is shared with every data point I see. The challenge for most people is that retirement is a huge unknown.

We know what we want…to be comfortable, cared for, and entertained…but find it very difficult to attach a price tag to all of that. And since I will draft retirement plans for clients as young as 20, it's next to impossible to forecast how your life will be in 35 years.

The good news is that nothing is permanent.

Once you commit to establishing a retirement plan, it doesn't mean that if you ever deviate from it you'll be sent to a penalty box for tampering.

But the reality is that many people avoid the planning or don't commit adequate time to it because it seems like such a distant reality. "I have kids to get through college first." "I'm not eligible for my pension until I'm 65." "I love my job so much I can't even imagine leaving it." People find many excuses to avoid long term planning.

The first thing I tell my clients is that if they can tell me the year they'll pass away, planning will be extremely easy! Unfortunately/fortunately we don't know how long we'll be around. The only reference we have is family history and I give that a lot of credence.

Why is retirement planning so important? Because we'll spend almost as much time IN retirement as we did working to get TO retirement!

Many people are living 30, 35, 40 years after retiring. Do you know how expensive it is to pay for 40 years of expenses without having a job?

So what are the important components of retirement planning and what needs to be considered in order to create a successful plan?

There are too many to list, but below are the areas I find most critical when working with my clients.

1. How much money do you currently make?
2. How much do you currently save?
3. What investments do you have set up solely for retirement (401(k), 403(b), Profit sharing, Defined Benefit plan, etc.)?
4. What "assured" income sources will you count on in retirement? Social Security, Pension, etc.
5. What do you want to do in retirement? Travel? Work part time? Volunteer in the community? Watch the grandkids?
6. Where do you want to live? How will your retirement income be taxed in the state you live in?

7. Do you have Long Term Care or any protection were you to end up in a nursing home?
8. What debts do you currently have and what is your plan to eliminate them?
9. Assuming you have assets remaining when you pass, how do you want to leave your legacy? Pass to family? Support a cause important to you? Donate to an alma mater for them to name the stadium after you?

These, amongst some others, are the backbone of information to help in constructing your MVP Retirement plan.

College Planning:

If instead of calling retirement planning the MVP, and instead calling it the captain, then college planning would be the co-captain. Not quite as important, but still pretty important.

Think of this: according to the College Board, tuition has increased by 1,120% since 1978. For comparison's sake, medical costs have grown by 600% and food costs have increased by 244%.

And then think of this: according to the New York Times, only 19% of full time students earn a bachelor's degree in four years. Adding more years just adds more to the bottom line cost.

Even at state flagship universities, only 36% graduate on time. What does that mean? You might be paying for 6 years of college instead of 4! And what about graduate school? Medical school? Law school? Who will pay for that?

How in the world does a family do that, while also saving for the MVP of planning, potentially putting more than 1 kid through school, and paying normal and daily bills?

I have a quote that states there are "Informed Buyers and Uninformed Buyers" when it comes to paying for college. Planning appropriately will help you become an informed buyer.

With two young kids of my own I am sharing the same fear, pain, angst and disgust with you. For that reason, I focus on college planning much more than many other financial planners. In my opinion, in order to become an informed buyer, you should consider these items:

1. What is the best way to save for college? 529? UTMA? Life Insurance? Retirement accounts?
2. How can I save for college while also saving for retirement? Is there room at the table for the captain AND the co-captain?
3. How does the financial aid process work? Free Application for Federal Student Aid (FAFSA), the Profile, etc.
4. What is my EFC (Expected Family Contribution) and how does it dramatically influence the way I approach college planning?
5. Why should I file financial aid forms, I make too much money?
6. How do I find the right school fit for my student?
7. How do I look for scholarship money and what resources are available?

8. What strategies (income, asset, and tax) are available to help me save ON the cost of college, not FOR it?

Other Planning:

I just discussed in some detail the two main expenses that clients need to plan for.

However, there are many others that your financial quarterback should be able to help you with.

I am not discounting any of these as they may be more important to you than the two above. However, for the sake of space I will quickly bullet some of most common goals (aside from retirement and college) I help people plan for.

1. Estate Planning
   a. How do you want your assets to be handled when you pass?
   b. How do you pass your money to your beneficiaries as efficiently as possible while keeping the courts out of the process?
   c. How do we plan around the state and Federal gift exemptions?
   d. What happens to my money if I get sick while I'm alive?
   e. How should I title my assets to make sure they are handled in accordance to my wishes? Real estate, businesses, investments, life insurance policies, etc.

f. Who will be my representatives to carry out my end wishes?

2. Insurance Planning
   a. How much life insurance do I need?
   b. What type of policy should I carry? Term, Permanent, Whole, Universal, Variable Universal.
   c. What am I looking to protect? Family? Business partners? Creditors?
   d. Does Long Term Care insurance make sense for me?
   e. What valuables do I own and are they adequately insured?
   f. Other than keeping me dry in a rain storm, what is an Umbrella (policy)?

3. Tax Planning Strategies
   a. How can I minimize my tax liability?
   b. How best do I structure my retirement income to avoid having all of it taxed?
   c. Should I use tax deferred, tax friendly, and/or tax free investments?
   d. Does my CPA work with my financial quarterback to make sure they're calling the same game plan? *Think of this as the offensive and defensive coordinators working together to beat the same opponent.*

4. Personal Asset Purchase Planning
   a. How much house can I afford?
   b. How much do I need to save to buy the lake house of my dreams?
   c. I need a new car in a few years, how best plan for it?

      d. I have two weddings coming down the pike, what do I do?

5. Business Planning
      a. What type of retirement plan best fits the needs of my firm?
      b. Should I set myself up as a C-Corp, an S-Corp, an LLC, or a Sole Proprietorship?
      c. How do I protect my family's business interests if I pass away?
      d. What team of professionals do I need to make sure I am operating in the most efficient and equitable way possible?

Game Summary

There are many points in your investing life where you won't be able to see the forest through the trees. Since the advisor has created not only a map of the forest but has a deep understanding of the trees in the forest, the most successful long-term client relies upon their advisor.

Now just because someone is a Financial Advisor doesn't mean they deserve carte blanch trust as I'm alluding to above. That trust is earned over time. Clients need to become comfortable with how the advisor works and believe in the process. When you enter into a relationship with an advisor, you should do so because you want to find a long-term ally and partner that you can rely on to help you through these emotional points over your lifetime.

Next time you watch a football game (if you even like the sport) I hope you watch how the quarterback plays a little bit differently. And the next time you're sitting in front of your Financial Advisor, I hope you're a bit more perceptive. Even though they are in two unrelated industries doing very different jobs, their goals are the same. In the end, they want to lead their teams to victory. For an NFL QB, that may be defined as winning the Super Bowl. For a Financial QB, that may be defined as guiding their clients to financial success…whatever that means for each, individual client.

Overtime

The opinions voiced in this material are for general information only and are not intended to provide specific advice or recommendations for any individual. All performance referenced is historical and is no guarantee of future results. All indices are unmanaged and may not be invested into directly.

This information is not intended to be a substitute for specific individualized tax or legal advice. We suggest that you discuss your specific situation with a qualified tax or legal advisor.

Investing in mutual funds involves risk, including possible loss of principal.

All investing involves risk including loss of principal.

No strategy assures success or protects against loss.

Acknowledgements

There are so many people to thank. I want to say thank you to my clients who have put their faith and finances in my hands, because without them there are no acknowledgements.

I need to thank the Pittsburgh Steelers organization for not drafting me to play for them. My failure to make it into the NFL has allowed me to enjoy a great career in the financial services industry.

I have to thank the first mentor I had when I started my business at age 22. He took me under his wing, educated me on how to listen instead of speak and helped me understand the value of our role. Bob Nyberg, thank you.

Even before my career began, I had two parents who loved, supported and encouraged me no matter what I chose to do. Tim and Debbi Williamson, I will be eternally grateful for everything you've done for me.

Since 2005, I've had two tremendous business partners who have been on this journey with me. They've taught me more and continue to teach me more than they realize. Thank you, Rick Shanley and Paul Fousek.

All of my team members over the years who have helped me with my practice. They do the heavy lifting behind the scenes that allows me to look good in front of my clients. Specifically, Kaitlin Wysopal has been the engine of my business for the past 5 years.

I want to thank Anna Rose Benson, a new incoming freshman at Michigan State University and a proud scholar recipient of The Legacy Guild. Anna Rose designed the cover of my book and plans to major in design and marketing in college.

This book wouldn't have been written without the consistent and persistent nudging of my professional coach, Jean Kuhn. Many thanks for staying on top of this!